Praise for *Hug an Angry Man* . . .

"Here is mind's soulful inwardness given lyrical expression—
a compelling story of a life-long search for meaning, and for
honorable, caring human connection."

ROBERT COLES, M.D.
Pulitzer Prize Winner
Children of Crisis
James Agee Professor of Ethics
Harvard University

"Leclaire's strong writing carried me into the entertaining,
moving, painful, hopeful tapestry of his colorful life. His
poignant stories and soulful poems take the reader through
the nitty-gritty stuff of a challenging life and a timeless spiritual journey."

ROBIN CASARJIAN
Author of *Forgiveness*
Director of Emotional Literacy Projects
Prisoners and Youth-at-Risk

"This is an incredibly powerful book. It can save lives, mar-
riages and relationships. Many millions will identify and
benefit from it. I laughed. I cried. It's all there."

FRED MILLER
Author of *How to Calm Down*

"These raw and incisive stories and poems are the path of one man's journey in search of his soul. For the hurt and angry men out there this book is a must read."

ALMA LEE
Artist Director
Vancouver International Writer's Festival

"*Hug an Angry Man* . . . is a compilation of profound and insightful stories, life experiences and poems that are at once heart-warming and heart-wrenching. It is a book that begs of you to look within yourself and welcome whatever you should find. This book is stirring and evocative!"

KARTER KANE REED
Inmate
Maximum Security Prison
MCI Shirley

"Sean Leclaire uses the gritty sand of his experiences to make beautiful glass; his stories and poems cut deeply as they shine brilliant patterns of light inside our heart."

LINDA HOFFMAN
Author of *Winter Air*

"From his poetry, rich sutras, and undeniable spirit Leclaire reminds us we are more than our story and that we are 'all branches on the same tree'!"

Menswork, Inc.

Hug an Angry Man
and You Will See
He Is Crying

HUG
an
ANGRY MAN
and
YOU WILL SEE
HE IS CRYING

Stories and Poems

SEAN CASEY LECLAIRE

RED SPIRAL BOOKS
CONCORD, MASSACHUSETTS

Published by: RED SPIRAL BOOKS
                  PO BOX 1101
                  CONCORD, MA 01742

Editor: Ellen Kleiner
Book design and typography: Dede Cummings Design
Cover art: Anja Borgstrom
Cover design: Dede Cummings Design

Copyright © 2003 by Sean Casey Leclaire

Printed in the United States of America on acid-free recycled paper

Publisher's Cataloging-in-Publication
  Leclaire, Sean Casey.
  Hug an angry man : and you will see he is crying : stories and poems / by Sean Casey Leclaire. — 1st ed.

     p.   cm.
  LCCN 2002095006
  ISBN 0-9724859-0-2

  1. Self-realization. 2. Leclaire, Sean Casey.
  3. Men—Biography. 4. Anger. 5. Recovering alcoholics—Biography. 6. Spiritual life. I. Title.

BF637.S4L43 2003   158.1
                              QBI33-812

10 9 8 7 6 5 4 3 2

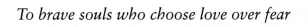

To brave souls who choose love over fear

*What has no shadow
has no strength to live.*

—CZESLAW MILOSZ—

CONTENTS

PREFACE

We all have stories. Colorful, cocky stories. Bland, boring, nothing happening stories. Horrid, sad stories. Stories filled with beauty and great achievement. But when our identities are linked to our stories—of people, places, and things—we are deluded. Until I surrendered to a deeper identity than my own colorful and sad story, I suffered. I failed to grow because although the scenery and characters changed, the story and lessons remained the same.

It seems that though we toss our troubles to the sea, they continually come back until we meet them with deeper levels of understanding and forgiveness. Then once we've accepted and learned the old lessons, we are graced with forward movement. A story that has never been shared is indeed a sad thing, but it wasn't until I gave up hope for a better past that I began to grow spiritually.

Along life's crooked road, I was blessed by the strangest angels, weird and wonderful people who taught me how to forgive and how to love. For example, the title of this book was inspired by a street person named John who pressed his wild heart into me one lonely and terrific night, as described in "The Hug." The title *Hug an Angry Man and You Will See He Is Crying* is meant to both ignite reflection and pose a challenge: Dare to choose love over fear—every day, every moment—even when it feels like your ass is falling off.

Working with coaching clients, I have learned most people like to take a few baby steps before they leap. So, if you are not up for actually hugging an angry man, consider a three-breath hug with someone you care about, or someone who looks like they could use an embrace. Choose such a person every day for a week, and after asking permission hold them heart to heart long enough to complete three deep easy breaths. Take this risk and you will begin to soften, becoming powerful like water.

I believe we live in a time when people are losing the ability to think reflectively and feel deeply, and thereby tap in to our spiritual nature. In response to the high value placed on progress, performance, and profitability, we rarely reside in our bodies anymore and may in fact be living in the first disembodied culture. Nowhere is this more evident than in business, where millions of individuals daily engage with pulsating screens for hours on end. Our bodies have become slaves to machines—entertaining machines, feeding machines, diagnosing machines, money machines, exercising machines, machines for love. Our flesh, our bones, our blood, sweat and spit, our "life juice" has nowhere to live. And, when we are not on fast-forward in the frantic serenity of machine life, we tend to drift back into the sad spin of our worn stories, failing to realize the power of this present moment and the fullness of embodied life.

I hope the stories and poems in this book will prompt you to turn inward—to laugh, cry, and maybe throw the book across the room. If being with these accounts inspires you to examine your own stories, including the untold ones, start letting go of those that have been shaping your life for too long. Forgive whomever you need to, and laugh more easily at yourself and with others. Very soon you will see that we are not our stories but rather more, so much more.

In one sense this book is a spiritual autobiography, though I think of it more as a door opening into green fields of love. I'm still on the edge closest to the door, for I am a slow learner in important areas: the surrender of ego, abiding trust in the wisdom of current reality, and the valuing of spiritual life over materialistic existence. But fortunately I am not the only one seeking awareness in this spiritual kindergarten.

See you on the teeter-totter!

INVOCATION

MEN COME IN THE ROOM

MEN come in the room. Mad men. Glad men. Been had men. Many men. Honest men. Drunk men. "Barely holding on, man!" Men come in the room. Men whose lives have been ravaged and wives have been raped. Men who have raped men come in the room. Pill popping. No stopping. Pussy hunting. Mushy men. Men come in the room. Barrel-chested hairy men. Scary men. Old men. Young men. Movie-going middle-aged men. Men come in the room. Bald Buddha-loving men. Fast talking. Bullshit walking. Still drinking. Coffee-pouring men.

Men come in the room. Men shoveling shit from their lives. Men without wives. Men who won't listen to their wives. "Gotta get that bitch back!" Men come in the room. Men without men in their lives. Gay men. Straight men. Horny men. Hungry men. Men who were once men. Men with cocks come in the room. Angry men. Anal men. "What's with that attitude man." Men come in the room. Guitar men. Gotta get the hell out of here men. Men with hurt bigger than mountain men. Broken token—just a shadow of a man. Men come in the room. Barely men.

Men come in the room. Doctor men. Lawyer men.
Ladies' men. "Who the fuck do you think you are, man!"
Woodworking wild men come in the room. Poor men.
Poet men. Porno men. Pot-spinning men. Men who have
spent more time with the devil than most men—real men.
Men come in the room. Money men. Toy-loving men.
Men who act like boys. Chain-smoking wheelchair-
rolling sober men. Soldier men. Saint men. Sinning men.
Only men.

Men come in the room. Crying. Lying. Dying men.
Men whose mothers were like men. Fatherless men. Men
come in the room. Big men. Soft men. Fast men. Lucky
and loose men. Troubled men. Hard-driving finger-
flicking never gonna stop pushing the river men. "See
you cocksuckers later, man!" Men come in the room.
Kick-ass and kiss-ass men. Bleeding in your bones men.
Liver- bloated heavy men. Skinny men. Men who can say
to other men, "Bigger trees have fallen at my feet, man."

Men come in the room. Men dragged across their front
lawns by men-in-blue men. Drinking, fucking, fighting
men come in the room. Raging, rocking, no-stopping,
truck-driving, boiler-making, metal-shaping, saxophone-
playing men. Skull-cracking men come in the room. Bad-
ass guns in the car men. Men come in the room. Messy
men. Married men. Scared men. "I can't breathe in here,
man!" Forgotten men. Forgiving men. Men with bowl-
like bellies, arms, and hands. Men with tree-trunk legs
and feet. Laughing men with big balls enter the room.

Men come in the room. Love you till you get better
men. Deep men. Men who love their women. Nondrinking

men. Jesus-loving men. Men-helping men come in the room. Gotta go back to school men. Tree-climbing, true blue men. Men trusting men. Men come in the room. Trudging the foothills of God men. Mercy men. Word-loving men. "Heard it first here, man!" Circle-praying men. Kid-loving men. Men come in the room and the soft innocence of men with men in a room comes in the room.

— I —

The Wound

*You are not the water
you swim in, only the
water you drink.*

DRY CHEEKS

Sitting at sharp wooden desks, with unanswered
   questions.
"Just do it this way," they said.
"Don't think."
"What could possibly come of that thought?"
"Be quiet. Sit down! Shut up!"
"I'll report you to the principal!"
The large brooding man had his own set of
   principles—the sharpest,
an eighteen-inch black leather belt, three quarters
   of an inch thick
and four inches wide.
At school, the principal stopped whipping when
   you began to cry.
At home, I was taught boys don't cry.

FIRST COMMUNION

Rage is a river.
You ask me why
love makes me quiver?

Skin cut and slivered
red on the thigh.
Rage is a river

Inside his roiling
red eyes.
Love makes me quiver

Down by the river
the sky
raging river.

The priest, he's the giver
with God-gorging eyes.
His love made me quiver!

Smile cold and shiver—
the cross-raising guy.
Rage is a river.
Love makes me quiver.

THE BURNING

DURING the first year of my life, Catholic Charities moved me every two months so the foster mothers would not get "too attached to the baby." I have no memories of these early road trips—only the hollow feeling I carry in my sad, dark Catholic heart. They finally hung my hat in Chateauguay, Quebec, close to a soon to be infamous Indian reservation called Kahnawake. There I quickly learned that Canadians call the native people Indians, not Native Americans. A drunk Indian, frozen dead in the ice, is just that—a drunk Indian.

The Iroquois at Kahnawake were trouble. For years they had been moved from district to district on the island of Montreal. They were integrated into our school system in the eighth grade. The second week of classes, Doris Goodleaf grabbed hold of Annie Jensen's long blonde hair and tossed her through the front office window because of something about Doris's boyfriend and Annie. I feared the Iroquois boys, who were strong and proud and wore their hair long with red bandannas, but I was head over heels for the Indian girls, who were loose and wild, drank Southern Comfort, and smoked. When you are thirteen with a bone-on a dog can't bury, Iroquois girls are a gift from the Great Spirit. Some were Catholics, like us, but most followed an old tradition called "Longhouse." My history teacher told me after class one day that these people, now a dying breed, had once been great warriors and the Iroquois culture and the wisdom of their ceremonial fires had provided the framework for America's Declaration of Independence.

Manhood in our town was determined by your ability to drink, fuck, and fight. I always thought you should get to know a guy before deciding to beat the shit out of him, but my friends and the Iroquois felt differently. Bruno, Birdman, and Big Willy got into frequent fights with Iroquois students, and during one lingering Indian summer Duke hammered three Iroquois who had jumped him after football tryouts.

Duke, whose real name was Stewie, and I used to fight in the sandbox. He was a tough kid who lived around the corner from me. His father had made him tough—the way a father can, and shouldn't. Because of him, I learned by age seven that when two men beat each other they could go to jail but when a man beats a kid it's called discipline.

Duke had gotten his nickname in the tenth grade when he threw the teacher, Mr. Mitchell, in an airplane spin out the second-floor window of English class. I wasn't there, but Bruno saw it, and Bruno always told the truth. Thank God he wasn't with us the night of "the burning," as it became known.

That day in mid-February began normally; it was just after Valentine's Day, when Duke's dad had spent the night in county jail for getting too aggressive with Duke's mother. Following tenth grade homeroom class, my friends and I dashed to gym for a much-anticipated floor hockey match against Boy Boy Norton and his two brothers and three cousins—all Iroquois students. The game was played with broken hockey-stick handles and a dark blue velvet ring, two inches thick and five inches in diameter. You poked your stick into the ring and, using all your strength, you pushed into the floor and took off toward the opponent's goal, whirling like a tornado.

Midway through the first quarter, Duke cross-checked Boy Boy into the stage. Boy Boy punched him and the two began slugging it out toe-to-toe. The gym teacher, Mr. Polinski, let it go for a while, probably enjoying seeing Boy Boy land so many punches to Duke's face after the incident with Mr. Mitchell.

Duke lunged forward like a wolverine, grabbed Boy Boy's head with both hands, and gave a forehead smash to his face. Boy Boy's right eye started to spurt blood, and all of us yelled, "Head butt, head butt."

Before Mr. Polinski could stop the fight, Duke landed another right to Boy Boy's jaw, causing him to drop bloody faced to one knee—but just for a moment before he quickly jumped up.

My stomach churned, but not because I was a pussy— that is, frightened. It was because I was secretly dating Boy Boy's cousin, Charlene LaFleur, and the Iroquois stuck together.

This fight between one of my friends and Boy Boy meant problems for me. For one thing, it could retard my sexual exploration. For another, I liked Boy Boy. And all the girls loved this kid, including our women. It was the way he moved and how he watched things. He had long silky black hair with rugged cheekbones, steady eyes, and strong legs. The muscles of his thighs rippled as he tore by us on the ball court. He was pure stallion.

This time it was his amazing recovery that ended the fight. The buzz in the hallways afterward was about how fast Boy Boy had landed the first three shots of the fight. Duke, however, didn't say a word the rest of the day. No one had ever before fought him to a draw.

That night, although it was twenty degrees below zero, Duke, Big Willy, Birdman, Hawk, and I went out in a field to drink a bottle of Mr. Cronin's 180-proof Newfoundland Screech that Hawk had stolen from his garage. Big Willy saw the Iroquois first. He was lying on the ice like an old seal. The Indian had probably wandered out there smashed. Or he may have been thrown out of the Freeman Tavern, owned by Bruno's father—a popular bar where a guy had recently gotten shot over an argument with two strippers, or peelers as they were called.

We approached slowly, as if coming up on a dead animal. Duke stood over the body, and kicked it a few times. He chugged a couple inches of the liquor and spit a mouthful in the guy's face. The rest of us circled him, speechless. Finally Duke held up the bottle and told us, "If you want another shot of this Screech, take it now. This red man is kindling, nothing but kindling."

No one replied, so he emptied the bottle over the guy, and with the skillful fingers of a much older man, struck a match and folded it inside his half-closed fist, allowing the flame to rise. Then he tossed the match onto the body in disgust.

It's not like we murdered anybody, but snowbound and

shivering, something in me froze with fear as I searched my mind for a fitting response to the situation. Having read in a social studies book that people in India burn the bodies of the dead ceremonially by a great river, I screamed, "Make it a ceremony." The body went up in flames. The more it burned, the quieter we got. We stood in the silence of snow, as the fire lit the darkness around us. To me, the burning felt like a prayer.

The others left first. I walked away in slow circles, to the squeak of fresh snow under my boots, rising into the stone-cold night. Duke stayed for a long time. From the top of the rise I could see him crouched like a wolf by the burning body.

Our weekly newspaper gave "the burning" full coverage. The front page featured a photograph of the field and the tavern, and I overheard Duke's dad remark while reading the paper, "The only good Indian is a dead Indian." The article stated that the Iroquois chief and our mayor were going to get to the bottom of this incident, but they never did.

The seeds of self-hatred were sewn for Duke by the beatings his violent father gave him and they were sealed on that forgotten night by the Freeman tavern. The smell of the Indian's burning flesh became an indelible part of me, arousing a feeling of frantic serenity, easily triggered by the striking of a match or the lighting of a candle. I first discovered this phantom part of me when twenty years later, during an infrequent winter visit to Chateauguay, my legs gave out as I fell against a parked car, gasping for breath outside the big shopping mall. Just yards from me was Boy Boy with three kids and a beautiful white woman who used to be a cheerleader for the basketball team in senior high. He was leaning against a red and white Trans Am with a cigarette in his mouth. He had just struck a match.

THE GOSPEL

Yesterday
I spit in the face of Jesus—
not the original one,
the one I bought
at the church bizarre.
This morning
I sat in church to say
I was sorry.
There were thirteen people in the pews.
Everything was cold and old—
dead men in suits,
ladies with painted-on faces,
offering one another peace
they did not have.
The priest, slumping in his chair,
could not stand at the pulpit.
All his piss and vinegar had run out,
the Good News
dying in his voice.

DOWNTOWN

I drank till my face hit the pavement
and did not understand
that years of sharpness had sent
the lack of a caring hand.

I stretch my dreams for dinner,
on this cold and creeping day.
The priests, they shaped a sinner—
with blood in my eyes, I pray.

BEST FRIEND

THE LINCOLN Town Car pulled up to the curb in front of the Palliser Hotel in Calgary, Alberta, and my brother-in-law Bill eased his hefty frame from the driver's seat. We were to have breakfast, and then he was going to drop me off at Molson Brewery's regional office to brief the sales force about the upcoming Molson Golden advertising campaign and gather regional support for a national television show I was producing about the sport of extreme skiing.

While strolling along the block separating me from Bill, I marveled at how my life had changed. I had quit drinking, my career was flourishing, and I was flying around the country giving presentations. Still, the friendships of my wild youth lingered like embers in a fireplace. Just the night before, I had gone to dinner with Brof, who had parlayed years of ski-bumming and periodic construction work into icon status at a local ski mountain. Hearing that I had given up booze, he'd refused to order his beloved Jack Daniel's.

"It's a good thing you quit. You get crazy when you drink," he declared, looking at me seriously.

"You're right, but I'm not the one who brought a goat with a pink bonnet to that party on Electric Avenue," I retorted.

We teased and reminisced the way we always did. Then I explained what it was like working in the white-collar world. "My first few years at the advertising agency were fun. But now I need to wear armor in front to protect myself from clients and armor in back to protect myself from colleagues."

"When you put on a suit and tie, I realized not all business goofs were pussies," Brof had said, laughing.

When I approached the Palliser, Bill waved me over to his car. "We'll just head up McCleod Trail and get a good cowboy breakfast," he said while we climbed in and eased away from the curb. I could only imagine what breakfast would bring. I knew from working construction in Calgary ten years earlier that July was the month of Stampede, the world's largest rodeo, a time when you could find even the most timid souls dancing on tables at downtown hotel ballrooms on Friday nights, and the hard partying often began at breakfast with eggs and whiskey.

We were driving slowly through a four-way intersection when my head was mysteriously turned by some unseen force. As a kid, my sister Julie and I had talked of angels and magic, but as an adult I had put aside such nonsense. Yet at that moment my gaze was unquestionably drawn to a large, filthy-looking man leaning against a lamppost, with his head drooped. When he just as serendipitously lifted his chin and looked right at me, I realized it was my best friend Bo, whom I had not seen in seven years.

"Stop the car!" I shouted, leaping out and running toward this big, ugly street person, no doubt convincing my brother-in-law I was crazy.

But Bo did not appear to know who I was; he stared at me blankly. I reached out to hug him, and his arms remained dangling by his sides even as I squeezed my chest into his. He was still a rock, just like when we were kids. Bo had been king of our high school. He could leg press over five hundred pounds and worked loading motor-oil engines onto freight trains. As a senior he was drafted to play professional football, then he hurt his knee badly and was told he could not play anymore. That's when he started drinking Coors, chasing whores, and hanging out with one-eyed Jack. Jack loved Captain Morgan's rum, poker, and young girls. He had been in and out of prison for shopping when the stores were closed.

Soon after, Bo and I left Chateauguay and headed west, where I had seen him off and on until seven years ago. By then his alcoholism and drug use had progressed, and someone told me he had been beaten half to death with a baseball bat in an alley behind Bradley's Bar on Crescent Street in Montreal—something about an old cocaine debt.

One time, Bo had shown up at my office in Vancouver unannounced, hair down to his butt, all jacked up with his goofy grin and a guy called Piglet. They were driving a baby blue Mercedes convertible and smelled like they hadn't washed in weeks. I was drinking then, too, so I left work early and partied late and hard, showing up at the office the next day still drunk. That was the difference between Bo and me: I had always worked, and except for a year of concert promotion, he had never held a real job.

Now, because Bo still hadn't said anything, I began wondering if he was mute as a result of his incident with the baseball bat. We stood there—him looking at the ground, me trembling—in that awkward kind of funeral silence.

After yelling at Bill that I couldn't go for breakfast and watching him drive off, I ushered Bo into a cheap-looking coffee joint with two grubby, white plastic tables on the sidewalk in front. I smoked and rambled on about my work and marriage, and how I had just seen the Brof. Bo listened, and every once in a while I was sure he would say something like, "Remember the Charlie Daniels concert, 'The Devil Went Down to Georgia,' Boz Scaggs, George Thorogood, and those two broads who were fighting over you?" Or, "Remember the night you fought Duke to a draw in front of The Bar Flipper and two strippers found you guys passed out in the graveyard with three empty bottles of Southern Comfort?" But he sat still as a Buddha.

With every breath a new memory from our childhood flooded my consciousness and I yearned for the closeness we once shared. I knew I could not stay with him much longer because a blazing fire was whipping through my blood and bones. It was Bo who had convinced me to go back to school and study media and public relations; he said I'd be good at relating to people. He introduced me to Mount Royal College pub life and many fine women and suggested I stop wasting my talent working concrete with Big Willy. Bo had been my rock during the difficult transition from itinerant construction worker to college graduate and advertising executive. In high school, he was the only friend I never fought with and was careful not to tell the others I had joined the chess club. He also respected that I spent a lot of my free time reading books, though while passing by the library after football practice, he would drop his drawers and press his big butt cheeks against the window, making me howl until I got kicked out. I watched all his football games and he cheered at my basketball games. Bo kept all the sports page coverage of my basketball exploits in a scrapbook. Once when I'd taken a cheap shot from a dirty player on the opposing team, Bo bolted out of the stands and three teachers were needed to peel him off the guy.

Staring now into Bo's eyes, I pictured him as a chubby kid whose mom died way too early. I saw him wide-eyed like the sun, beaming with his MVP football trophy, and later holding my girlfriend's hand when they were king and queen of the Winter Carnival. Feeling harsh rain and giant trees falling inside me, I excused myself and dashed to the men's room. But barely had I made it to the back of the restaurant when I burst into tears and began wailing like a mother carrying her dead child away from a terrorist attack. I returned to the table a few minutes later with an image of Bo standing stage right of Boz Scaggs, wearing a navy blue peacoat and white silk scarf and reveling in the concert he had produced.

Knowing there was an American Express office on 4th Avenue where I could get Bo some money, I hailed a limousine and got in the backseat with him. While staring out the window, I heard him softly say, "Nice ride, Fast Man. Ain't been on a nice ride like this in a while."

Other than Brof, no one else in western Canada knew

me by that name, a moniker Bo had given me in the ninth grade because he was certain I could beat Minnesota Fats at pool and knew I had gotten caught with my pants down helping Debbie Wilson with her math homework, whereupon her unhappy father had chased me down the street butt-naked in mid-January.

"It's good to see you, Fast Man," Bo mumbled, a little louder.

I remained breathless for the next three blocks, so happy that Bo was still alive, that inside he was still there.

After we reached the American Express office, I asked the driver to watch Bo, as I dashed to get a couple hundred bucks' cash on my Amex card. When I returned, Bo was not in the car.

I pounded on the driver's window. He pointed toward the alley, where Bo was semi-squatted, hands on his knees, head tilted down. He was taking a crap with his drawers still up. All he said was, "Didn't want to mess up that nice ride of yours, Fast Man."

— II —

Resentment

*Resentment is the poison
you pour for another
and drink yourself.*

CLOSE TO THE BONE

No one
needs to live this way:
An ugly meager dump,
shit-faced man
slumped on an old blue couch—
fingers fumbling on shotgun,
death dark,
sobbing.

Suddenly
fluttering wings:
Two angels softly on body breast,
working angels
with feverish laughing eyes—
one on the heart,
the other
burning.

REHAB

They said,
"First things first.
First you stop drinking, then
you look at why you drank."
I thought,
"Fuck you and everyone
who looks like you."
They said,
"Keep coming back, it gets better."
I thought,
"Better than what?"
Fuckin' booze.
I always drink.
I drink to be alone.
I drink to be together.
I drink so that when I fight
I can't feel, and when I fuck
I do not cum.
Drinking, fighting, fucking—
it's a profession.
They said,
"Easy does it."

I thought,
"Who came up with this shit?
Some old guy, some ancient
   motherfucker,
some New Age conehead?"
I hate this place.
Why did I come here?

DRUNKS

I AM not my past or what has happened to me.
This basic truth was poignantly driven home to me
during a luncheon at the Tea House in Vancouver, British
Columbia, with two friends from a twelve-step recovery
program. I arranged the luncheon after Rick had slipped
again, getting "struck drunk" as people in recovery say,
and had called me in a breathless panic. I was at the end
of my rope with Rick, having tried everything: kindness,
tough love, thought-provoking conversation, even threats
of beating him into sobriety. The truth is, recovery programs are not for people who need them but for people
who want them—desperately. In the hallways of recovery, you hear a lot of clichés, which turn out to be true:
"Stay with the winners," "Don't drink and you won't get
drunk," "Think before you drink," "Easy does it," and so
on. From watching folks in recovery, I learned primarily
what *not* to do.

Despite my frustration with Rick, I had a strange fond-
ness for him. Earlier that year he had broken months of
silent scorn and shared at a meeting, proving he could be
witty. He had said that when he was initially trying to get
sober he was so sick he actually thought I was the West
Coast distributor of wellness!

After Rick's call, I decided that maybe the wise old owl
Jim, known for his calm perspective, could help Rick

weather his current storm. I did not know much of Jim's story, but I liked how comfortable he was talking about his love of Jesus, and how he kept things clear and concise. I was like Gandhi with a shotgun when it came to supporting men who asked for my help, while Jim conducted himself with no hint of impatience.

Waiting for Jim and Rick, I sat on a bench in front of the Tea House. It was spring, and the cherry blossoms and hundreds of red and purple and white tulips provided an uplifting fragrance and easy serenity for our meeting. As the two men approached, the difference in their attitudes was clear from their movements. Jim walked softly, while Rick stomped along, leaving traces of his anger in the earth. Jim, an unassuming-looking man, stood about five foot five and wore an old rumpled gray suit with his tie undone down a couple inches and running shoes. He gave the impression of being an unsuccessful accountant, although I had no idea what he did for a living, which is often the case in twelve-step programs. You know the most intimate, terrific things about a person but not where they work, or even their last name. Rick, nervous as a jitterbug, was a big man with thick hair black as coal, a barrel chest, and an angry scowl. His belly was a large bowl of grief, holding experiences that had been swallowed but only half digested.

The three of us were ushered to a table on the veranda. After we ordered, I commented on how I used to attend a great luncheon meeting here on Tuesdays that my sponsor, Frank, had told me about. Everybody loved Frank, but nobody knew him—a one-man joke machine who later died sober. Before approaching me, Rick had asked Frank to be his sponsor, and Frank had said in his inimitable fashion, "No thanks, kid, you're a loser." Frank was not one for idiot compassion.

Jim and I munched on salads as Rick lit the first of many cigarettes and whined about his girlfriend and how horribly his dad had treated him as a kid. Rick believed it was his father's fault that he had turned out to be unemployed, to have a pill-popping wingnut girlfriend, and to be an angry drunk. I knew from experience that Rick could cut a "poor me, poor me, pour me another drink" tune with the best of them.

Jim tapped his fork on the edge of his salad plate as if about to give a toast at his favorite niece's wedding, but I knew he was not about to ask Rick and I to kiss. Rick stopped whining midsentence, then Jim began speaking very deliberately.

"You know, by the time I was three years old I was looking for another home. Most weekend nights, my father would come home drunk, stumble up the stairs, and beat me with his belt. When I was in the first grade, he started fondling me. Things progressed from there.

"On my ninth birthday, my mother prepared a wonderful dinner of spaghetti and spice cake, my favorites, and promised that my dad would come home sober and would bring the Big Bruiser truck I'd been asking for all summer. Dad did not show for my birthday dinner. I ate very little of the meal, and my mother tucked me in bed crying. Late that night I was awakened by a noise in my room. My father, drunk, was dragging my mother across the floor by her hair, the way my sister Rita would some-times drag her Raggedy Ann doll.

"He pointed to my mother, facedown at my feet with cuts and red welts on her face and thighs, and yelled, 'Here's your cock-sucking Big Bruiser. Happy birthday, boy.' I never saw him again."

As Jim finished, he reached his hand across the table and said very softly to Rick, "Shame on your father for making you the way you are, son. And shame on you for staying that way."

I felt the wind move through a stand of willows by the pond just off the veranda. Rick said nothing else over lunch and left before dessert. Jim and I enjoyed our hot pecan pie and the silence of deep empathy as elegant swans floated by on the pond.

When I thanked him for talking with us, Jim offered some advice that still vibrates in my being like an old blues song: "One day that guy might be lucky enough to hear the pop, and that will be the day, God willing, that he finally pulls his head out of his ass! Let him go, Sean, you can't *get* him clean and sober."

Jim went on to become an active member of our fel-lowship and a city councilor. Rick, however, caved inside himself. He drank again and again, and is probably dead. Or worse, maybe he met a woman clinging to a horrible story of her own, and the two of them, groping in the dark, made a baby.

As for me, although at times I have felt like the bucket my family dumps its shame into, I believe that if I am willing to face my shadow projections and trust in the benevolence of current reality no matter how intense the shit-storm is that I might be facing, then there is nothing anyone has done to me, or I have done to myself, that the grace and goodness of a loving God cannot make as pure as winter's first snow.

THE SHADOW

This crazy part of me
staying up all night
hunting women,
sad women with hoping eyes
and strider thighs . . .
This crazy part of me
dangling from rocky crags,
laughing like Lucifer . . .
This crazy part of me
eats thick red meat
and pisses on family
cars in church parking lots.
This crazy part of me
smashing heads of business
on back-alley dumpsters
and living homeless
just to see if they know
something we have
    forgotten . . .
This crazy part of me
scares trees when he
    walks by,
and he wants to drink again

and hang himself from an
old train bridge.
This crazy part of me
does not understand
I have changed.
That is why he wants to
kill me.

BETRAYAL

Under an equinox moon
our cautious hearts cracked
open in the granite chapel
of commitment, and

I mistook you for the lush
asparagus of the farmer's field,
green sky-towers, ripe,
and I came diving to die.

I mistook you for my mate,
entwined and freefalling,
feathers and heat, beak and claw
under the soaring sky.

I mistook you for the snake
cool and curled on the coastal
rock of family history—
its skin never shed.

I mistook you for my she-bear,
our cub safe in the cave, as

you lumbered, marking territory
only you could wander through.

I mistook you for a mountain,
and you cast your shadow
on my dreams, skeleton-bone
woman.

CROONERS

Harvey had a face like a bad road. And his life wasn't exactly on cruise control. He slept under a wooden bench, out in the garden behind my condo; and when it rained, he would call me from a pay phone on the corner, announcing, "Ole Harv's getting soaked out here, man."

I met Harvey at a twelve-step meeting downtown. "The Nooner" was an eclectic gathering of folks that brought to life the truism you hear in the program: Addiction is an equal-opportunity destroyer. Five days a week at noon, housewives with their knitting needles, downtown doctors, lawyers, corporate power-brokers, and homeless people like Harvey, gathered to share their experience, strength, and hope—and to stay sober.

Harvey had taken an immediate liking to my rugged ramblings; my no-nonsense talk and the fact that I wore nice suits also impressed him. Although sober, he wasn't clean. A fiftyish crack-head, he was about six foot four, lanky, intensely blue-eyed, and an ex-boxer. "Went three rounds with George Chevalo, the Canadian heavyweight contender who got pummeled by Cassius Clay," he told me proudly after a meeting.

After most meetings, Harvey would make a move on me, pumping his fists and grinning as he asked, "Hey, man, you wanna be my sponsor? Come on, I need a tough guy like you. You've seen some street life." I did not respond to his banter. I was a busy advertising executive with no time for this loser. It was difficult enough getting away for these meetings, and the thought of hanging out afterward with God knows who was too much for me.

Soon, however, I remembered that a kind older man who helped me in the beginning had said never to refuse someone who asks for help. So I began mulling over the possibility of going for coffee with Harvey. You can break your heart helping people like Harvey, but that might be the whole idea—cracking open the heart. Getting sober is a long journey into the heart. And it takes time, earnest desire, and tender nurturing to regain the ability to feel and find new ground to stand on.

Harvey and I may have come from the same side of the tracks. But while he was still walking on the old side, with the help of good friends and sane direction, I had crossed over.

One Thursday Harvey came into the meeting late and noisy, as only an addict desperately seeking attention can do. He was really down, having failed to get a bull hunk position—slave to the camp cook, the lowest job you can have on an oil rig. I empathized with his situation since I had worked the rigs in summers to put myself through college, losing mobility in some fingers after laying heavy beatings on a couple of aggressive roughneck lifers who thought I was just a college kid.

During the meeting Harvey seemed to sink into a depression. While a woman named Jennifer was sharing, he began babbling. When she gave him a nasty look, he screamed, "Fuck you, bitch," then put his head on the table, no doubt mistaking it for a countertop at some cheap liquor joint. For the duration of the meeting, he kept looking up and mumbling like a man who had sat too long on his bar stool.

After the meeting, I saw Harvey pull Jennifer into a headlock. I lunged toward him with both hands, grabbed him by the front of his old down coat, and threw him ass-first over two dining tables. As he lay on the floor with an embarrassed look in his eyes, I smiled at him and asked, "What happened to that right hook, champ?"

"Fuck you, Sean," he replied, refusing the hand I offered him.

My crafty old sponsor said that I had to agree to be Harvey's sponsor since we had become so intimate. And so I did.

Harvey and I hung out together for several months, and for a while he got better. At first he kept bugging me to go to his part of town, then one evening I agreed. The two of us walked about twelve blocks onto his turf—past Eddie's Tavern, the Marble Arch (where you could see gentleman's ballet), pimps and prostitutes, piss tanks, and Catholic Welfare workers. Harvey finally directed us to a cheap karaoke bar, where he seemed to know everyone. "The bartender is an ex-con who used to own a hardware store, and our waitress, Stephanie, used to be a peeler before everything began to sag," he explained. Nearly everybody he talked to, or about, was a used-to-be.

I recalled how I used to be a student, and before that a roughneck on oil rigs, and before that a railroad tie gang-laborer, and before that a concrete construction worker, and before that a pool hustler—lots of things I never wrote home about. I had been sober a few years, and with each one the jobs and the company I kept improved. Harvey and his barroom friends were headed south and I was tracking due north, yet I still felt at home with them.

After two Coca Colas and a lot of bullshit, Harvey pulled out photographs of his five good-looking daughters.

"Where are they, Harv?" I asked.

"Don't know, man. Lost track a few years back. You know how it goes." Then he winked suddenly, swept his arms up like a vulture, and said, "Hey, Seanman, you want to belt out a tune with me?"

"I got no voice," I told him.

"That's the whole point, man—the machine helps you. Let Ole Harv show you how it's done."

He walked up to the karaoke machine working his cowboy boots like a man who had ridden some of life's tougher trails. Once on stage, Harvey began to sing: "Ayme, what you gonna do? I say I will stay with you, for a while, maybe longer, if I knew . . ." It was a verse from "Ayme," a classic country-and-western tune by Pure Prairie League.

Shivers ran up my spine as Harvey sang, smiling at everyone in the bar. Seeing them listening intently, I was sure something important was happening. In that precious moment I saw Harvey's gift to the world. I felt his sensitivity under the rough exterior and the beauty of his exquisite voice entered me, and I opened to the sadness of his story. When the song ended, Harvey bowed graciously, and everyone clapped. He was the lead man in the band that night.

To my horror, Harvey proceeded to inform the audience that his sponsor would now sing a song with him. "Seanman, just follow me and read the words. We'll be great," he assured me as I reluctantly stepped forward to join him.

He began singing the words that scrolled across the screen in front of us: "You never close your eyes anymore when I kiss your lips. I'm trying hard not to show it, but baby, baby, you know it. We've lost that loving feeling, woah, woah, loving feeling. Bring back that loving feeling, now it's gone, gone, gone, woah, woah, woah. . . ."

It felt as if we were in a concert hall and the people had paid to hear us sing. As we belted out the next verse together, Harvey, obviously pleased by all the attention, beamed with a radiance that I had never before seen on his face. Suddenly tears streamed down my cheeks, for it had dawned on me that Harvey was probably not going to make it, just like so many others who were unwilling to feel the pain of their untold, sad stories. I realized, too, that while my friend Harvey mediated his grief by living the life of a drifter, I was still hiding from mine in the sleek movements of the advertising world with its boardroom bravado and its powerful persuasion of public perception. It seemed that neither of us had yet surrendered to a healing power greater than our stories. Seeing Harvey's glow in the spotlight amidst my tears, I began to understand that my life was none of my business, and that I could no sooner get Harvey sober than I could keep myself clean and sober. I saw that real recovery from addiction was not an act of will but a gift, and that although I had many nights under my belt without booze, I was still hiding.

When we finished, the bar went wild. People came up and thanked us for our uninhibited sharing.

As Stephanie put a couple of free Cokes on our table, she said, "If he'd clean up and get a job, I'd marry the crazy bastard!"

Harvey leaned over and gleefully whispered, "Broads love crooners!"

— III —

Turning Inward

*Pain is the touchstone of
spiritual progress.*

IF I STOPPED

If I stopped for a year
to read the classics
what would happen?
If I stopped for a year
to visit art galleries and museums
would I ever work again?
If I stopped for a year
to dance and climb mountains
would the boardroom bell
not sound for me?
If I stopped for a year
would I learn who I am
in the angry eyes of our tender youth?
If I stopped for a year
could I feel the seasons change
and hear ants talk?
If I stopped for a year
would I learn how to breathe
and wake up the senses
I have long since forgotten?
If I stopped for a year
could I remember the birth canal
and the bright, white light called life?
If I stopped . . .

LOST

Sadhu—
Man of the East
Wanderer
Holy man
Teacher
Seer
Lover of the
Self.

Sadwho—
Man of the West
Drifter
Hole-in-the-man
Student
Seeker
Lover of
self.

THE HUG

I KNEW I was in trouble when my advertising firm acquired the most sought-after client in the Pacific Northwest and I felt empty, like I had just eaten a dime-store candy. What had formerly gathered my energies into a frothy fury of success now seemed to leave me cold and depressed. The previous fall, in Hawaii, I disappeared before a client's closing conference banquet where I was set to give a rallying motivational talk to their sales force. I simply could not rise to the occasion. Returning home, I began to write spontaneous, emotional poetry—verses that tightened a chronic knot in my belly. One night I made my wife nervous by apparently bolting upright from a dead sleep and screaming, "This dog's out!"

A few nights after we were awarded the new contract, my wife and I hosted a dinner party to celebrate the firm's victory. Midway through the evening, I tired of telling corporate war stories and slipped out of the house unnoticed. I walked along the beach feeling a flicker of panic as the ocean's brooding womb washed over my boots. My thoughts turned to the poetry I had been writing and the contrast between what some of the words were pointing to and the chatter of the advertising world. I began to think about how poets live—often on the outer edges of society, with an appetite for the unknown. The unknown, for me, had recently invited an inward turn toward healing repressed pain from past experiences and a focus on the shining peaks of faith I sensed growing inside myself. A line sprang into my mind as I shivered in a spray of soft rain: "Forgiveness begins in the green fields of love."

I wandered for hours, finally stopping at a twenty-four-hour bagel joint, where I ordered a sesame bagel with cream cheese and a cup of steaming latte from a sassy young woman with streaked purple hair. While carrying the food upstairs to a small dining area, I noticed on every table a thin white candle, the kind you hold between your fingertips during midnight mass. The ambiance seemed peaceful, with only one other person there. So I took a seat at an empty table, planning to sort through my feelings of alienation.

Immediately the other diner stomped toward me on what appeared to be a wooden leg or foot, or something. Under his right arm he held a crumpled-up plastic bag from Denny's. The guy sat at my table, unrolled a sloppy old burger that stuck stubbornly to its wrapper, and, chomping on it, barked, "Hey, you want a bite?"

"No," I answered abruptly, glaring at him with resentment for intruding on my late-night latte.

Seemingly unfazed, he reached into his coat pocket and, one by one, began pulling out soggy french fries layered with dried ketchup.

It was hard to determine his age, as is true of most street people; the guy appeared to be between thirty-five and sixty. He was ugly, smelled bad, and had his gaze fixed on me with an eerie Charlie Manson glare. Insisting on conversation although it was 3:00 A.M., he bent his head toward me and blurted out, "My name is John— from the Montreal area."

Like this mattered to me. This guy probably wandered west to escape Montreal's brutally cold winter and screw up my late-night latte.

I decided to ignore him, hoping he would wander off.

"Did you know that *dog* spelled backwards is *God?*" he asked.

Again I did not respond.

"Did you know *dog* spelled backwards is *God?*" he challenged, more loudly.

I picked up my steaming-hot coffee, thinking that if he leaned in any closer I could throw it in his face. But he just kept staring, like some night-owl skitzo.

"Did you know that . . ." he began once more.

"Yes, yes, John. I know, I know," I finally replied, hoping to ward off further dialogue.

"Then if *dog* spelled backwards is *God,* he must be man's best friend. Right?"

"Right," I answered, managing a weak smile. I asked him if he had a dog and where he lived.

Bowing his head, he growled, "Ain't got no home. Ain't got no dog. Ain't got nothing."

For some elusive reason—perhaps wanting to help a stranger because I had not been able to help my best friend Bo—I wrote down my phone number, saying, "John, why don't you give me a call sometime, and we'll go down to the pound and get you a little god."

The guy's face, toughened most likely from too many

dumpster dives, softened for a moment. Then he smiled as big as a kid hearing the ice cream truck.

While the candlelight flickered on our faces, I felt a tear well up in the corner of my right eye. Rarely one for tears, I flashed on the two times I could remember crying: while singing with Harvey at the karaoke bar and as I sat with Bo at the coffee joint. John must have sensed my unfelt pain, for he suddenly whispered, "We are on the same tree, you and me, just different branches."

Touched by his tenderness and terrified that a deep and sad river might come crashing through both of my eyes, I got up to head for the men's room. But John lunged forward, banged his chest awkwardly against mine, and wrapped himself around me like a boa constrictor, burying my face in his chest. With his heart beating like a wild drum, the man was hugging me, holding me up, and refusing to let go. Heat raced up my spine and swirled through my neck, my throat opening like a tunnel. I wailed like a lost boy, arms limp at my sides.

After a few minutes, John folded me into a chair. Nothing was said. I stared into the flickering candle flame, then disappeared to the men's room to gather myself. When I returned, John was gone.

I sipped the rest of my latte in a state of awe, mystified that a guy as socially awkward and physically repulsive as John could be such an athlete of the heart. I was astonished that he could stay whole before my waves of grief and see the necessity of unraveling my pain in his embrace. Awakening, perhaps for the first time, to healing fires of intimacy, I smiled as the words of a spiritual teacher rippled through my mind: "Go ahead, light your candles and burn your incense and ring your bells and call out to God, but watch out because God will come and he will put you on his anvil and fire up his forge and beat you and beat you until he burns brass into pure gold."

Thankful that John had hugged me back into my heart, I vowed never to forget that just beyond loneliness and terror there is beauty.

DIRGE
(For W. B. Yeats)

There is the weight of Sunday afternoon and
the sadness of rain

There is the choking of unspoken words and
the wailing of ancestors

There is the horror of homeless huddled at noon and
the yearning of women

There is the crying of tea waiting to be poured and
the emptiness of a cup

There is the whine of cattle fattened on sheep and
the lying of businessmen

There is the poverty of spirit shot with cocaine and
the dryness of water

There is the loneliness of a breeze with no face to kiss and
the scream of an oak, cut

Junah says Jesus was nailed in a storm and
the Second Coming is already here.

JUNAH

He has been my blood since the
    beginning.
The strength of his hands was formed
on Egyptian stone block.
He stomped his fury with Genghis,
and drank with Alexander as
    Persepolis burned.
He held an enemy's heart in his hand
and ate it—
the bitter taste of civilization stinging
    his mouth.
He was a king long before kings were
reptile-like men ruling
from skyscrapers.
He is the roar of the rose
in the early morning heat,
the falcon grinning
at Shogun's feet.
He is the song in Philemon's tower.
When he breathes,
ancient forests sway and bow.
He's the crazy horse circling
the outer edge of the inner circle—
the one
chanting by the forbidden red river

the one
playing the green violin
the one
burning in the lake of sorrow
the one
with two white cobras on his arm
the one
who carried the carpenter's son
when the boy was lost in the East.
Junah
is the man women want
and hope won't stay long.
He is the shape of steel.

YOGA

After coming to realize that I spent my waking hours persuading people to purchase things they didn't need—things that turn into stuff, stuff that turns into junk, junk that clutters their lives—I began looking for someone to manage my advertising agency. I needed a break from the trappings of my Ralph Lauren life: first-class travel, five-star hotels, exotic vacations, a luxury condo on the ocean, and famous acquaintances I called good friends. I was every bit an American success story if you ignore the fact I was overweight, restless, irritable, and discontent. As the poet Leonard Cohen says, "I was aching in the places I used to play."

After one particularly draining sales trip, I woke before dawn with a phrase circling my mind: "Worry is the interest you pay on fear." Over the last year, I had become aware that my identity was completely linked to the fact I was the founding partner and president of an advertising firm, and that although I appreciated the success of hard work, I did not enjoy the pretense, utter greed, and narcissism of the corporate world. I was starting to feel like my soul had turned into steel; and each time more poems poured into my consciousness, I became increasingly worried about what the hell was happening to me.

That morning as light began to peek through the windows, I decided to soothe myself by walking the beach.

The air was fresh and still, the tide pulling back from the rocky shore. In the distance I saw a lovely, seemingly young woman arching her back in strange, evocative positions. As I approached her, intrigued, I could hear deep resonant sounds coming from her throat that reminded me of Darth Vader, but this woman did not appear aligned with the dark forces of nature; on the contrary, she emanated grace and beauty. Amazingly, as I drew closer I could see that she was in her fifties. Sensing my presence, she folded in on herself like a shy swan, clasping her palms at her chest with her head bowed. After a full minute of silence, she raised her head and smiled at me.

As the sea wind gently caressed us, the skin on my arms tingled and my face was flushed like the red sun ascending on the horizon. I was a lumbering 220-pound corporate executive accustomed to barking out orders and making people jump, and yet in the presence of this woman's focused energy I was silenced. She tossed her towel over her shoulders and said to me, "Yoga," as if that one simple word could resolve all the dissatisfaction with my life. As it turned out, yoga opened the door for inner exploration and a healing I could never have imagined was necessary, much less possible.

Living as a professional actor does, in and out of roles, I came to yoga as a man of many masks. They protected me from a past I was unwilling to face and loath to feel, as well as a career I viewed with growing skepticism and disgust. Prior to founding my own company, I had apprenticed with a brilliant and bombastic mentor at an international advertising agency; and I still remember with horror, sitting in a brand management session realizing I had constructed the boardroom floor—less than four years earlier. My rapid advancement from trudging in gum boots, knee-deep in wet cement, to having an elevated job in the slick advertising world was too much for me to fathom. That night, I went "off the wagon" and got struck drunk. I ended up in a barroom brawl and spent the night as a guest of the men-in-blue who claimed I had kicked one of our city's finest in the head during the fight. The next day, I had to get a close friend in the agency to bail me out so I could make my flight to Los Angeles for a Molson Golden television commercial production.

Taking up yoga while suffocating beneath my various masks proved interesting. At first I did it the only way I knew how—as if running a fly pattern on the football field, or doing wind sprints during basketball tryouts, or running stairs at track practice. I was pumped. The approach worked for about two years, then my left hip started to hurt.

During this time, I was often awakened in the middle of the night by poems penetrating my consciousness. It was like energy inside me reached up from the dark sea of my unconscious and insisted I write. After jotting down a poem containing the phrase "business is a rabid white dog with no eyes," I began to accept the possibility that my advertising career was coming to an end. While having lunch a week later with the Sport Network's vice president of programming, for whom I was producing a television show about extreme ski racing, I blurted out that advertising changes people's simple wants into dire needs and told him I was through. Despite what appeared to be a fabulous life, I had crashed my ship on the reefs of power, prestige, and possessions.

Right away I started looking for someone to run my company for a year, thinking that after years of striving to achieve a certain amount of professional prestige, I would take a well-deserved trip around the world. An associate of mine expressed interest in managing the company during my sabbatical, but a month after we signed the deal I was still showing up at the office. Having no identity other than that of "big boy boasting in the boardrooms," I could not let it go.

So my body took over. I got pneumonia and eventually pleurisy, which was like breathing razor blades. And yet from my bed I was still making calls to the manager of the company, explaining how I would handle various deals. One night, after finishing the last chapter of *Re-Invention of Work* by the renegade Catholic priest and Creation Spirituality pioneer Matt Fox, I collapsed on the floor in breath-stopping pain and, following a dash to the nearest emergency room, passed three kidney stones.

Resting in bed a few mornings after, I wrote: "If you scratch lust, you will find utter loneliness; if you scratch utter loneliness, you will find emptiness; if you sit with emptiness, you will know God." But the God I remembered was the God of the priests, and like a lot of recovering Catholics, I was loath to enter those unholy waters again.

Then I met Svaroopa Yoga pioneer Rama Berch, who taught me that 90 percent of physical pain, including the chronic problem with my left hip, is fear provoked, and that yoga is not an athletic endeavor but a spiritual science leading to an unfolding of consciousness capable of inspiring significant personality change. Studying yoga with Rama Berch was similar to standing by the ocean and saying to the spirit of the waters, "Rise and fill me." Spirit came to me. It is in the divine's job description that when we ask, we receive; the problem is that the ego gets in the way and edges God back out of our lives. So I tried to keep my ego from intervening, which was as futile as trying push away ocean water.

Although Rama's style of yoga had a lot to offer I wasn't ready for her teachings. I subsequently indulged in "watch your neighbor yoga," participating in numerous athletically oriented yoga workshops. I had been so conditioned for competition that I did not even notice how much I drove myself to be as good as the person next to me. The lingering, aggravating hip pain helped me notice.

I fought the pain, which persisted for another two years, like the good soldier I had been taught to be. I gave up golf and basketball, substituting Reiki and Rolfing, massage of all sorts, rollerblading, shiatsu, acupuncture, osteopaths, and every body-centered therapy invented in the last forty years (with and without primal screaming) at about $100 an hour—a costly adventure. I even had a drunk Russian shaman bounce me around my loft for an afternoon, hoping to ease the pain of what New Agers call AFGO, another fucking growth opportunity.

Nothing worked. Between periods of minor relief, I still seemed to be wrestling a thirty-foot python, resulting in frustration and soon panic. I began having heart-thumping panic attacks. It is very hard to remember that "this too shall pass" while convinced that you are swallowing your tongue and God has forgotten you exist. Panic can kick your ass. At such times, I wished that the inner guides I had read about in books with the word *soul* on the cover, would magically appear so I could bend some angel wings.

One panic attack began on the Monday morning marking my return to Vancouver after nine months on the open road hanging out in ashrams, Benedictine monasteries, studying with monks, yogis, and shamans. I had begun to change—having shaved my head, lost forty pounds, and become conversant in spiritual matters—but the darker parts of my mind were still seething. In retrospect, I realized, I had essentially become just another sick, angry fuck hiding in the health-food store aisles.

On Monday morning I crumbled breathless to my knees in the living room, with my fingertips trembling and my toes turned to ice. Suicidal urges and thoughts pounded my mind relentlessly; storm waves crashed on the shore of my very being. Flames scorched my spine. My belly pumped orgasmically as I shrieked and sobbed like a baby. Eventually I pulled myself up, using a chair for leverage, and paced the living room. Seeing my reflection in the mirror, I did not know who I was. With a stabbing pain in my chest I went to the car and began driving through the neighborhood, now also not knowing where I was. Whatever had been holding me together had broken. I turned hot, cold, then I mumbled and prayed, "God grant me the serenity to accept the things I cannot change . . ." Braking suddenly behind a car stopped at a red light, I noticed its license plate, which read, Terror.

The irony of this event made me alternately laugh and cry, releasing me from the grip of panic. I wondered if the emissaries of light arranged such coincidences, if these angels had engineered all the turns necessary to bring me behind that particular car in a hairy moment of panic.

Over the next couple of years, the more I opened, the more I fought change—and the more I suffered from panic attacks and pain. I had not yet weathered enough of life's turbulence to understand, and more importantly to trust, the teaching that nothing really happens to us but rather it all happens *for us*.

My awareness began to deepen when I engaged in a series of yoga teacher trainings and body-centered therapeutic certifications, something I had never imagined doing for a living. Initially I was sure that if my mind did not need my body for transportation it would have eliminated it long before. But a smart-assed New Age friend brought me to my senses, telling me, "The mind needs the body for transformation as well as transportation." And it was Rama Berch who brought my attention to the deeply held pain in my body. Her style of instruction had been influenced by years of living with a yoga master in India and the need to heal her body after a series of car accidents that occurred upon her return to America. As such, she emanated compassion, and engaging with her intellect was like taking a sip from a fire hose.

The more I practiced with Rama, the more I began to relate to my muscles more as angry ghosts than broken machinery. While driving home from yoga class one day early on, I felt my low back burning intensely, and abruptly the electrical system in my van melted down, emitting a puff of smoke and a whine—a perfect metaphor for the state of my inner landscape, I thought. But as time passed I could focus on a deep, unchanging state of being for the first time in my life, feeling a sea of sensation inside me. During one particular class, the pain in my left hip diffused into a sensation of grabbing, then heat, shifting eventually to coldness. Icy, bitter tears ran down my cheeks, and my fingers and toes felt lined with jagged, blue edges. As my mind grew still, I was able to explore these sensations further.

"You tapped into the core of your spine," Rama said, lovingly, when I told her about them. "Your inner core is frozen, and there is so much tension along the spine, from your tailbone up through your neck and into your face and skull, that your beautiful bald head is beginning to point at the crown. Here is what to do. For a half hour each day lie on your back and do the Ujjayi breath. This slow throat-concentrated breath will settle your nervous system and give your mind a sound to focus on. Then practice the Magic Four poses to open the tailbone, sacrum, low back, and the more than two hundred muscles attached to the spine. Do this every day and your hip will stop hurting."

Feeling defensive, I tried to dazzle her with my vast knowledge of yoga, whereupon she replied, "Just do it. See for yourself." It is strange how we take the time from busy schedules and pay good money to a teacher, then try to impress them with how much we already know about the subject. As Robert Frost said, "To learn anything new, we must go by the way of ignorance."

Soon my ignorance opened the way for learning. I stopped thinking and gave up fighting my body and mind, following Rama's instructions every day for the next six months. My pain did go away. But more importantly, while lying on my back for half an hour a day, with my knees propped up by blankets as I paid attention to my breath and body sensations, I learned a great deal about how repressed events in my past had caused the contracted energies in my body. I came to realize that recovery programs and talk-therapy are only a beginning. That to truly heal, we must be willing to feel; we must release the blocked energy and unexpressed emotions living in our bones and muscles.

Next, I expanded the daily practice to 90 minutes and incorporated short body-centered breaks into my daily routine. Taking a two-minute break and doing a spine-opening lunge or forward bend silenced my mind's chattering, figuring, and fear-filled plotting long enough to let me experience the sensual bliss of being in a body. It was like traveling to a foreign country I had always wanted to visit. Coming in contact with the emotional release at the source of a chronically contracted muscle taught me that, as the prophet Bob Dylan sang, "behind every beautiful thing there is some kind of pain," and that pain can be a touchstone to spiritual progress.

— IV —

Relating

*It does not matter who you
are with, only who you are
when you are with them.*

INNOCENCE

Northern India.
Rain coming in sheets.
A million miles from anybody . . .
The rainbow color of your eyes—
How long have we?
And now your body, sculpted of Rodin,
is wet and tall, and I am fifteen again
and oh so fragile
touching your butterfly cheek.
Laughter fills the room.

LEARNING TO WALK

She tells stories
forgetting I was there.
I go places
forgetting who she is.
I crave the deeps; she likes
the safety of surface things.
She is smart.
I am intelligent.
She likes *People* magazine and knows
directions to Walmart and Lucy's Diner.
I ponder Pluto, sunflowers, and rocks;
she knows how to get from A to B
and that Pluto is a planet
far away up there.
She is afraid of the dark;
I've been swimming in it for years.
"Look baby," she says,
"I'm a cable station.
"You are a freakin' satellite dish."
We are both still walking on one leg.
Reaching to hold each other, we fall down a lot.
The problem is, we are in love
and kindness is still a concept.
It needs feet—
two each.

ROAD TRIP

THE BLUE sky spilled stillness as I walked barefoot on Summerland Beach near Santa Barbara, California. The surface of the sand was winter slick, and hard, yet I seemed to be trudging through deep weeds. Ginger Mahrone and I had finally ended the push-pull dance we'd inadvertently choreographed.

I could think only of her at the ocean-side apartment, with its old ironing board by the computer, psychology books scattered on the kitchen table, cowgirl boots by the door, a silky yellow print dress draped over the chair, laundry folded and stacked on the other chair, magic markers spread across the coffee table, and colorful lists in her day-timer.

Even now, alone on the sand, I could feel the warmth of her chest like a hundred suns. I had felt both safe and turned on with Ginger, while normally it was one or the other with a woman. With Ginger I sensed a deepening as together we learned how to stand in love—not fall in love like kids or romantically challenged adults—and have different experiences with the same partner instead of the same experience with ever-changing partners.

Ginger had touched the moist and tangled parts of my soul. And our road had been filled with the treasures of new lovers: lingering conversations, dreaming, candlelight dinners, waltzing naked in the rain, tender healing, and the passionate turbulence of a proud woman shaped by men and a Scorpio man raised by women.

Last Monday night as we lay exhausted in messy sheets, Ginger blurted out, as only a thirty-eight-year-old woman can if she is living with the terrifying tick-tock of I-am-never-going-to-have-a-child, "Things are different when you are looking for the father of your children."

I pulled away like she had let go a bad fart. "Hey, you want to have a baby, don't you," I exclaimed, with an acute grasp of the obvious. "Look, *I'm* a freakin' baby!"

She laughed, no doubt amused that a forty year old who had just had his first butterfly tattoo inked into his right shoulder could see himself as a baby. But I did.

Since starting yoga I had experienced healing waters churning, yet transformation takes time. Until recently, my body had been like a garden hose riddled with kinks—mind kinks. Recognizing that human experience contains a certain amount of suffering, I opted for useful suffering (pertaining to the soul's desire to purify and unite the mind and body) over the useless variety (which involved succumbing to endless criticism from the gremlin mind). But on some days my gremlin mind, flooded with fear, would morph into a six-hundred-pound gorilla, grab me by the scruff of the neck, and smash my body against telephones poles, a phenomenon that occurred with increasing frequency during my growing intimacy with Ginger. I could commune with God on the yoga mat, but not with Ginger over the dinner table.

Having a baby, I thought, will kick my ass! But heaven help a man who gets in the way of a woman set on having a child, especially if she's a redhead like Ginger. Instantly we got in one of our fights. Then with her voice still burning in my ears—"Sean, you're living proof that a person can still be an asshole after *samadhi!*"—I marched out the door, climbed into my '76 Dodge van, and hit the road.

The blue van (BV for short) was my steel womb.

For two years prior to meeting Ginger, I had wandered bareback with a backpack on the dusty roads of India and Indonesia and then lived in relative silence, cruising the back roads of America with the Western canon packed into the side panels of BV's bosom. It was a time of lying fallow, writing, and getting lost in the power of reflection.

BV and I rode together, with no destination in mind. We wandered far and slow, like lonely rivers. I would rub her affectionately every once in a while, and she would listen to my stories, even when I cried like spring rain. I learned to take showers standing in gas station washrooms, and we found out every service station owner in America is named Joe. We wore out our first pair of tires in the Southwest, becoming friendly with the crack of dawn, wandering for days without memory, and watching angels make wild wing streaks across the cool, black sky.

On a mesa by the Chama River in New Mexico, while looking for Christ-in-the-Desert Monastery, BV picked up a Cherokee woman, and by nightfall her dress was up around her hip bones, her muscular limbs moving like water, her heart howling like a she-wolf as she watched a circle of fire. Although she soon went west, I stayed a month at the Benedictine monastery, filling the days with prayer and thoughts about becoming a priest. After that, BV and I headed toward the City of Angels looking for her and got lost in a neighborhood where the only white folks were those smiling on freeway billboards. While playing some bad-ass-white-man-can-jump hoop, I broke a finger and BV lost a tire. We never found our Cherokee friend.

We turned east again and in Bakersfield, we hit hard rain and wind. BV slowed to 15 miles an hour, and we could barely see the turbines turning on the hills. We pulled in by a tattered cross, ready for sleep. But when we learned no overnight parking was allowed at the adjoining Prince of Peace Christian Monastery, we stole Jesus and took him with us, leaving those monks struggling in their robes.

In the Sierras, we signed up for spiritual boot camp, joining mind-maddened men dressed in discipline. BV rested her worried frame, while I practiced yoga for 16 hours a day, chanted the Bhagavad Gita (yoga's bible) and meditated for 120 days, going goddamn nearly insane. BV honked her horn in protest the day the good swamis began talking about me taking vows of celibacy and wearing an orange robe. We made a U-turn and headed southeast, eventually singing loud songs in clapboard churches throughout the Bible Belt; swinging north, we realized the road to hell is paved with the skulls of predatory priests.

In Washington, DC, I got a massage from a three-hundred-pound black woman named Lucy, who while finishing looked up and said, "Boy, when you smile, it makes me all juicy!" We stayed a while before hitting the road again, slipping in and out of old bookstores in small towns, making friends with Socrates and Sappho, Rilke and Rumi, Wilbur and Jung. We read every book we could find on psychology, spirituality, or the new science, and wore the cover off the poetry book for men entitled *The Rag and Bone Shop of the Heart*.

We rode and rode and read and read—and ran.

Months later we stopped at a Vipassasana Meditation retreat in northern California for ten days. "Simply sit," the leader said. "Sit with the memories." My thoughts tossed and turned like roiling sharks as I sat in a room full of seekers, body aching, knees crying, mind like glass, breathing in, breathing out, day in and day out, sitting silence, walking silence, washing dishes silence, sleeping silence, dreaming brown robes of priests, hard cocks, lips, pubic hair, the church library, books, a door handle, a river, the red sky.

Still walking Summerland Beach, I gazed toward the sea, watching pelicans along the shoreline and slipping into a meditative state. Suddenly three shimmering beings appeared before me. Shaped like mythological seabirds, they had emerged from the atmosphere like rainbow trout surfacing from a muddy stream. I blinked, came out of my meditative state, and thought, "Oh my God, I must be hallucinating!" I shook my head but nothing changed.

Although many things I'd witnessed and experienced in my life had made me fearful, I had no fear of these luminous beings. And, although my legs buckled somewhat, like a once proud flag on a sailboat tacking a windless sea,

I remained standing, motionless. Mesmerized, I watched as the celestial creatures sent sounds in my direction. Entering me the way a man enters a woman he adores, the tones formed words: "We are proud of you, my son." Such words were never said by my father, though I had longed to hear them, as all sons do.

I reflected on the legacy of most men I meet—sons of sons with sons in silent dark rooms, not reaching out to each other, not expressing their true feelings—and on my own as well. Of my two dads, the first, whom I never met, apparently raped my birth mother and left in a hurry. The second, the one who adopted me, virtually lived in his workshop and often told me, "You got two thumbs for fixing things." He hugged me with his heart wide open once, six weeks before we buried him.

After telepathically offering these cherished words, the celestial seabirds moved slowly and silently up the coast, with the grandeur of mountains moving over the ocean. And I added their gift from the unknown to those I'd received on the road trip. I was now fairly certain of three bits of crazy wisdom: God allows U-turns, everything is subject to change without notice, and until a man can accept love and tenderness from other men, he remains incapable of loving a woman completely.

THE FOUR SEASONS RULE

Millions of men and women
   stumbling
fumbling into one another's front doors
   with bags full of wanting,
looking for a safe place to unpack their
   baggage.
The "I love you" wears off, and they
   start arguing about
where the baggage belongs. Marriage
   can seem like war.
I have decided to implement a new rule:
After a relationship ends, spend four
   seasons alone.
And, if I move to California, two Los
   Angeles Lakers seasons,
including playoffs.

HEALING

The blood-soaked grace
of Christ entered me,
and what once ran cold
flashed fire, blue storm,
and the earthbound heat
of a red, red rose.

TEACHER

F ATHER Placcidus and I became fast friends. His deep kindness and keen intellect appealed to me, and I imagine my fierce but friendly soul amused and invigorated him.

After the years of wandering, my attempt at reentry into society was hard. Fear kept pulling me back into the corporate world, while my heart and soul wanted to write plays and poems and continue traveling. A friend suggested I might find comfort in the solitude at British Columbia's Westminster Abbey. So I arranged to stay there with the Benedictine monks, under the spiritual direction of Father Placcidus.

I came to the abbey with a troubled mind and restless heart, flip-flopping like a fish out of water. I told Father Placcidus about Ginger and the possibility of settling down and becoming a father; he thought marriage was a fine idea. I remarked that he was supposed to say such things and knew nothing of the travails of marriage; he said he was married to Christ, a most demanding and difficult bride. I laughed, finding such a notion tough to disagree with!

Placcidus pissed me off. Real spiritual teachers do that. Their words often strike like thunderbolts, or they won't answer my questions and instead ask questions I cannot easily answer.

One hauntingly, beautiful twilight while I was sitting under the cherry tree near the chapel door, Father Placcidus leveled me with an insight as we deliberated about my life choices and direction.

"Well, Father, I am considered a genius in the advertising world," I ventured with the cocky air of a frightened man.

"Son, it must have been easy to rise to the top of such a mediocre world," he replied.

Father Placcidus's wisdom wounded my ego.

My ego did not like to go to monasteries and chant, or to practice yoga and meditation—unless I could tell people about it and win admiration for my rigorous discipline. Nor did my ego like to serve others or admit to not knowing something. Only further up the mountain of awareness would I learn that an acknowledgment of ignorance can be lifesaving while wrestling with Truth, which for me was like nervously trying to nail a hundred pounds of Jell-o to an oak tree.

Along infinite paths up the mountain, my teachers had taken many forms. I got blissed out with some, blasted by others, and blessed by a few. The best pointed to the light, while helping me face and befriend my shadow. Father Placcidus was bringing the light of consciousness into the darker parts of my personality and teaching me that kindness kicks ass. Disagreeing on many aspects of his religion, we debated. I told him that priests raped some of my friends in elementary school and also tried to rape me. He told me that priests are not the Church, not the body of Christ.

I used the words *fuck* and *Jesus* in the same sentence and told Father Placcidus that I prayed with my middle finger flipped to the sky. He said, "Jesus takes prayers any way he can get them, son."

He advised me to praise everything the divine put on my plate. Then he showed me how while making a big deal of *anything*, I was making a big deal of myself. "Just your edgy persona flaring up again, Sean," he would say.

The anger and the tears were so interconnected I never knew which emotion was going to come out first. During one of our sessions I got so angry, I could not breathe. Awash in bitter tears, my fists striking the air, I managed to blurt out, "Sometimes, Father, I feel like my heart is breaking."

"That's how the light gets in, son," he replied.

I wept. He wept.

We sat side-by-side wrapped in silence, two pebbles in a cool running stream, washed by a power greater than themselves.

— V —

Toward the Light

*God is writing straight
with the crooked path of
our lives.*

GOAT MIND

Cliff
    watching the sun
    descend into the collarbone of night.
    The steel guardrail saying,
    "Not beyond here."

    The man thinks of his wife and baby boy,
    heavy thoughts, of how the family shattered
    like rock against a hard sea.

    Goat mind springs forth,
    propelling his body over the sheer
    take-your-breath-away rock and the

Heart
    Ready as rain
    pours down, down, and down
    the massive mysticism of stone.

    Perched on a ledge no wider than his footprint;
    the rock gives way; flung-back arms and hands
    grab for God; the sound of boots scraping,

the solid things of his life
falling into the sea's throat.
Spine cold as creek water.

Fearful like an animal,
his right leg snags
an old root, midair, the man

              dangles

like a snake.
Goat mind kicks in.
The peregrine falcon floats by,

his mercury heart knocks, and
the great door that does not
look like a door

Opens
   "Climb."
Climbing.
Climbing!

              Goat mind is wild mind.

Wild
    mind is no mind.
    At thirty feet, blood begins
    to pump up the thighs again.

    Climbing man, crying, leaps to an outcrop,
    and squats, the seawater shaping the soft face
    of his wife before the storm.

    The man slides down
    the black slab of night,
    his feet softly touch the beach sand.

    The mountain creek
    flowing into the salt sea
    bears a newborn light.

HOMECOMING

I want to crawl
into the womb
where the imprint
of my personality
shines in the dark
with God's laughter.

LEPERS

IF ANGELS could drink, Singh's mango lassi would be the unanimous choice for the morning toast to the gods, I thought, drinking one as I squatted by the side of the road in Madras, India, seeking spiritual awareness. It was in the hustle and bustle and poverty of India that my mind began to slow down. And I started to understand that I would not be returning to work in the business world.

Drinking only local fruit juices until the midday meal and squatting were changing the deep muscle contractions layered through my hips, upper thighs, and pelvis. Feeling relaxed this close to the earth, I noticed that the softness of sunrise had given way to a sharper light. And later—amidst carts creaking, sacred cows defecating, the brewing of chai tea, store owners sweeping shop doorways, motor-rickshaws revving up, passing trucks laden with vegetables, and kids playing along the dusty streets— there was no neon, thank God, no signs of America and her beacon CNN.

Singh and I shared a love of Gandhi and his practice of *satyagraha,* "holding to this truth." Singh had told me about Shiva, how he became the greatest god, and Agni, who mediated between man and the gods. He had explained with great pride how he had been saving for a pilgrimage to Shiva's home, Mount Kailasa. With chagrin I realized how most of my "pilgrimages" over the last decade had been to the foot of some woman or to the marching orders of another corporate deal.

At midday, Singh shared the *dhal* soup and *dosa* (paper-thin pancakes made from lentil flour) his devoted wife had prepared for him, which we ate in silence. I felt comfortable in my own skin in Singh's loving presence. Our friendship was easy and the laughter full. I brought many questions to the keen mind and warm heart of this wise old street peddler. Singh taught me not to surrender my loneliness too quickly and to stop looking for God. "God is not he, God is not she, God is energy. Open your eyes and be," he would say and then giggle like a two-year old filled with the pulsating joy of daily living. The rigor of our conversation and his fierce devotion to his beloved Shiva opened my mind to the possibility of simply *being with* whatever was arising in the present moment. A frail man, with a puckish grin, he had the still eyes of a cobra and the courage of a lion, and like Gandhi, he served the poorest of the poor with the same reverence he engaged everyone who stopped at his fruit stand. During the last morning I spent with Singh I played marbles with three competitive homeless boys behind his fruit stand. We laughed so much it hurt. Singh's parting words were: "All is coming, question man. All is coming now!"

While wandering the streets after sunset, enjoying the banter and bark and market mischief of petty thieves and aggressive hawkers, I came across an abandoned construction site, where only two floors of concrete had been poured and all sides of the building remained open to the warm night. I stepped over metal tubing and pipe, and noticed a young boy playing in a large pile of sand. Seeing me, the boy scampered behind a ghostly wooden crate draped in plastic.

The moon was so low that the earth's heat had turned it into a glowing orange orb. Silhouetted against this backdrop on the second floor, I saw about a hundred people, leper families and other untouchables, crouched and lying by a dozen or so small fires. I climbed the stairs, approached slowly, and bowing while pressing the palms of my hands together at the center of my chest, said, "Namasté," which means, "I honor the light within you." A three- or four-year-old girl with raven hair and obsidian eyes, and wearing a tattered dress, moved shyly toward me like a young swan. Wrapped around her thumb and forefinger was a thin brown string to which was tied a one-eyed pigeon.

Intuitively I knew to sit cross-legged and wait. A man whose nose had rotted away, and who had no fingers but instead dirty white tape bunched down to the knuckles, brought a small plastic crate for me to sit on. I contemplated tossing it over the side of the open-air building to let him know I needed no special treatment, that I was okay sitting on the concrete floor like the rest of them. But I sat as requested, not wanting to offend him.

Accustomed to traveling first class in foreign lands, selling my wares and dining at the best American hotels, I was unprepared for the scene that followed. One by one, as in a B-grade horror movie, the lepers moved toward me and sat in a continuously widening circle. An old man told me apologetically that they sold marijuana, the village well had dried up and the only work they could get was as drug dealers.

We talked as best we could. He then introduced me to a girl blind from leprosy who climbed onto my lap, where she perched most of the night, never saying a word. A thin, regal woman in a beautiful purple sari sat across from us, the orange moon encircling her head. She radiated a fire of love that the furious pace of worldly commerce could never dampen.

I could have been robbed and tossed over the side of the building by these veterans of survival, for surely they saw I was wearing a money belt and probably guessed it was filled with cash and traveler's checks. But no one so much as asked for a penny; on the contrary, they exuded an abundance of their own. We laughed uproariously and sang songs. They were impressed with my ability to chant in Sanskrit, and together we praised many Hindu gods. I then set the blind girl on the ground, entertaining the kids with headstands and Donald Duck imitations. Watching a mother nurse her baby while leaning against a pillar, the child tucked securely against her smooth dark breast, anger flashed through my mind at the white man's murder machine and insistence on "progress."

The next night I was eager to return. At dusk I brought ten large vegetarian pizzas from my hotel, two buckets of ice cream, and jugs of water. This time, since word of my visit had apparently spread to the streets, the building was swarming with lepers and untouchables. I gave a village elder one hundred dollars but felt cheap and confused handing him the money. Afterward we had a pizza party, then everyone slept. Curled on the concrete floor, I felt caring hands rubbing my back and I instinctively muffled an urge to cry.

In India, I believe I was given an inkling of why Jesus chose to break bread with the unwanted and the dispossessed. During my morning with Singh and two all-night vigils with the leper community, I was able to see and taste and feel that God is good. So powerful was this infusion, it never occurred to me that certain strains of leprosy are contagious. More importantly, I came away from the experience not with anger over another distressing romance or business contract, but with bright images of a little girl transporting her one-eyed pet pigeon and a man presenting a plastic crate for his guest to sit on. To me, these people were holy men and women.

It was Mother Teresa, a saintly woman from Calcutta, who said, "You can do no great things, only small things with great love." Now when I reflect on this wisdom, an inquiry wakes me in the night: Why, when Mother Teresa and Princess Diana died that terrible autumn, was so much more attention paid to Princess Diana? And I think, perhaps it was because most of us want the riches of privilege, because most of us want to live the life of royalty and cannot, while every one of us can live the life of a saint—and will not.

STAR DUST

Burning
like jewels
sent
from a star's center*
we fall
into form
to taste
the holy honey
inside
as we begin
our wonderful wing
stop in the green fields
of love.

AWAKENING

Trust is deeper
than love.
Trust lives in and
outside of time.
Time is a steel trap
door.
Trust and emotional scar
tissue are kissing cousins.
Time and trust
are mad lovers—
time after time
the heart struggles.
Truth is a pathless land.

THE SEEKER

I RETURNED from India filled with soul-brimming awareness and the half–baked knowledge and spiritual pride of a beginning seeker. Despite awkward silences of old friends who were wondering what had become of the bombastic, hard-charging advertising executive they used to know, I opened a yoga studio in my home on Kits Point in Vancouver.

I had learned from my spiritual quests that God meets us halfway on the bridge of life and our job is simply to show up, put one foot in front of the other, and align our will with divine will. And I was beginning to understand that "free will" meant I was free to decide in any moment whether to act from fear or love. My goal was set: I would strive daily to choose love over fear, trusting that God would show me how to proceed and I would become quiet enough to listen. But although headed in the right direction, I did not yet understand that a little knowledge is dangerous and that I had unwittingly cultivated a spiritualized ego: I believed I was further along the path than my friends and family, and silently looked down on them. The ego preening itself on spirituality makes for a ridiculous spectacle among those who can distinguish its masquerading from the true center of our being. A teacher of mine ventured, "Everyone is crucified by his own ego, Sean, and you are no exception," but I suppose I had to find out for myself.

One morning, while most of the city headed toward bustling hallways of commerce, I stapled 3 by 5-inch promo cards to telephone poles near Starbucks on the heavily trafficked corner of Beach and 4th Avenue, fighting a hard sea-wind to keep the cards from littering the street. The cards announced that I would be teaching yoga classes in a loft apartment around the corner.

The contrast between my present situation and my past identity was a mind-twister. Previously I had owned a company called The Marketing Warfare Group, with a barbed wire design on our business cards. I had presented promotional marketing lectures to MBAs at local colleges, excelled in the guerrilla wars of national brand marketing, and managed the worldwide advertising for a $2 billion-dollar corporation. I had played golf with Arnold Palmer and Lee Trevino; stayed at Robert Trent Jones Jr.'s ocean-front beach house in Kauai; and employed about eighty-four crack-shot professionals on my last major event production, a black tie gala for 1,850 and the opening ceremony for the world's largest tourism industry conference. And now, in the same neighborhood where my ex-wife and I had owned a $500,000 ocean-side condo, I was about to convert a loft apartment into a combined yoga studio and home. I was going to get paid to help people to relax and slow down. I really had to give my head a shake some days.

Over the next few months many folks came to my yoga classes. They arrived tight, tired and frightened, and left calm and hopeful. I also took on private clients, published articles about spirituality, and gave talks about living in the body instead of treating it as an object. I sincerely wanted people to experience *illumination,* to know the bliss of their own being.

All the while, I continued having shifts in awareness. While looking at a patch of brown-eyed Susans in a friend's garden one morning, I disappeared into the petals. Three hours later I returned to time-bound reality, still standing in the same spot. Similarly, on a hot afternoon while tending potted tomatoes on the loft balcony, I touched a slender green stalk lightly with a forefinger and saw my hand dissolve into energy, then merge with the stalk as if they were streams flowing into each other.

Periodically I experienced other strange "openings," many of them bizarre energy movements accompanied by sounds erupting spontaneously from within me. I climbed a sacred volcano in Bali, naked and barefoot, chanting in a language I had never heard. A photographer friend took pictures that show a strange look in my eyes. He told me the villagers said I was a holy man, something I had to laugh at. The Persian psychologist I was seeing thought the "light of spirit" was pouring through me in response to my years of yoga, meditation, writing poems, and the deep cleansing of powerful crying.

Some days I walked about like the lens of a camera: open to everything, without thinking or feeling. My senses, soft and acute like rose petals after rain, would allow streaming energy to pulse through my skin. At such times I experienced the bliss of being in a body and felt as if I had entered the foothills of God.

Now and then, though, God moves across our lives like a wild storm, like an Inferno, sending us a wake-up call via harsh reality. Such an incident occurred while I was on my way home from seeing a client I had been coaching at his office in downtown Vancouver. It remains so vivid in my memory that it feels like it is happening now . . .

I'm seated in my Jeep during rush hour at the busy intersection alongside St. Paul's Hospital when an angry homeless man on wooden crutches approaches the crosswalk. As the light turns green, he tosses his crutches into the crosswalk and hobbles toward them. But instead of picking them up, he flops his frail body to the pavement and sits motionless like a stone. Then raising his head, he grips the edges of the crutches in either hand and begins propelling his rakish frame forward. Drivers in the waiting cars stare in amazement as he drags himself on his behind through the crosswalk—a North American leper in our urban twilight. Blood begins to trickle from his knuckles as he scrapes and pulls himself along. Horns blare; the guy stops three-quarters of the way across and, looking up, spits on the hood of my vehicle. Gazing into his eyes, I see a man broken with rage and disease and I know I have to act. Most of us have moments when everything becomes still, some preciousness moves through us, and we know just the right thing to do. At this moment I know to get out of my car and help the man cross the street. Spirit, calling from inside the man, is urging me to be fearless and help my brother—a man dying and homeless less than one mile from where I live. Instead, I follow the crowd and drive off.

Crossing Burrard Street Bridge, I feel shame, pure

shame. I park the Jeep in front of the loft and drag myself upstairs to my bedroom listening to the crack of thunder. I wish I had not turned my back on the man in the crosswalk. I know that streams of time will not wash away my refusal to heed the call of Spirit and hug this angry man. Then my heart cracks wide open, for I see hope surfing on a wave of grief, and I realize there are no holy men, only holiness healing broken men.

IN GRATITUDE . . .

STORIES and poems come to me from living in the white heat of life, and I do my best to recollect and shape these energies in quieter moments, which would be impossible without the support of loving friends. I am blessed to share a deepening intimacy with my dear friends Terry Ayers, a man among men, and living proof that white men can jump; Blasé Provitola, a true heart warrior and a brother with tree-trunk legs and soft hands; Linda Hoffman, an exquisite artist whose passionate spirit shatters glass; Lloyd Resnick, a lovely man who embodies compassion and common sense, and as the frontline editor, helped me begin to shape the manuscript for this book. I also thank my mentor and dear friend Patrick Thornton, who supports me in showing up and engaging with current reality.

With deepest love to my mother, Ellen Rosalie Leclaire, who has always been there—not an easy task for a good Catholic woman who adopted a wild child. To my father, Louis Leclaire, an artist and man of peace. To my youngest sister, Bin, and her boys, Tommy and Joey, for ongoing support and laughter (Habib says "hi"); my sister Julie; and my sister Lorraine and her kids.

Writing this book finally allowed the lingering pain of old wounds to fall from my plate like a feather and helped me open to the brilliant toddler joy of my baby boy, Beau Leclaire. In deepest appreciation to his mother, Sarah.

With devotion and the utmost respect I praise my yoga teacher, the indomitable Rama Berch. I came to you an angry man with his tailbone tucked under like a whipped dog, and you saw my magnificence and I love you.

I honor Father Placcidus, Father Austin Fleming, Garbis Dimidjian, William Emerson, my daughter, Jackie Sumner, Sandra Sammartino, Bradley Vettese, Tim and Sheila Dupuis, Howard, Roxanne and the kids, Jens Nielsen, Sandy Ayers, Lu and the O'Connell clan. I hold in the memory of my heart Stew Shearer and Dave Moore, who left this world too early.

To my fellow yogis and friends: Britt Sondergaard, Jonathan and Kathy Glass, Elizabeth Bunker, Fred Miller, Ron Kearns, Debrah Rafael, Lissa Fountain, Sophie Wadsworth, Sita, Shoshana , Maria, Maureen and the gang at Yoga For Life & Healing Essence, and J.D., Leo and the wild bunch from the Southside Keg in Edmonton, Alberta.

Thank you to teachers and poets Michael Meade, Robert Bly, James Hillman, Czeslaw Milosz, Mary Oliver, Sharon Olds, William Stafford, Allen Ginsberg, Robinson Jeffers, and Zen mountain dweller David Streeter, from whom I borrowed the phrase "You are not the water you swim in, only the water you drink." And where would we be without Hafiz, Rumi, Rilke, LaLa, and Sappho!

I am forever grateful to my editor, the brilliant Ellen Kleiner, who walks softly with a gleaming sword. She gave my lyrical passion and rhythms a structure so that the manuscript became readable. Let's create another book!

To the woman who designed this book, Dede Cummings: Your aesthetic sense is stunning. And thank you to Anja Borgstrom, for the magic man on the cover.

To my first agent, Amye Dyer: I enjoyed our time together. I am eternally grateful to the passionate poet and dynamic teacher, Harvard poetry professor Susan Carlisle. And I remember with appreciation the kindness and encouragement I received from Patti Gift when she was at Random House.

To my dear friends in Vancouver and Chateauguay— Jan Hamilton; Jackie Grad; Mike O'Shea; Bobby Brown; Lindsay Paxton; Michael Goehring; Pia Sillem; the Kitsin gang; Jan-the-man; "the King" Bobby Roy; Hawk; Swamper; the Devil; Mad Max; Trevor, Muck, Elvis; Big Benny; Ken McClure; Crazy Charlie; Birdman; Bruno; Ken "the Stroker" Crooks; the Fraser sisters; my first love and Jackie's mom, Linda Sumner; and my main man, the Brof: "You can take the boy out of Chateauguay, but you will never take Chateauguay out of the boy!"

Peace to the MacCrellish clan, especially Bill, for his financial support, and to Elizabeth Duvivier, for her encouragement when I had the idea I could write a book. And thank you to Ray, Kay, and the reference librarians at the Concord Library.

To my yoga students and coaching clients: Working with you provides me inspiration, balance, and courage, as well as a "day job" that affords me time to write. Blessings to my coaching colleagues, especially Stephen Carr; Francesca; Morgaine Beck; Ken Mossman; and my fiery and loving coach, Cynthia Loy Darst.

To the men and women who took time from their full schedules to read the manuscript and provide encouragement: Your kindness moves me and affirms the spirit of generosity.

To Harvey, John, Barry (Bo) Cushing, and the increasing homeless of this tear-stained world: There are more and more of us waking up, and we will help. You are not alone.

The invocation to the book, "Men Come in the Room," is dedicated to the men of RMOKOS (The Royal Mystic Order of the Knights of Serenity). I love you guys and thank you for coming in the room and continuing to enrich my life. Thank you, David and Patrick, for reading the manuscript in its rough form, and Barry and Jim, for your support.

The poem "Star Dust" is dedicated to Michelle: I am blessed to have recognized you, darling. We burn more brightly together. Ribbitt!

I acknowledge and honor the timeless and formidable warrior Junah: I kneel with my sword at your feet!

ABOUT THE AUTHOR

SEAN Casey Leclaire is an inspirational speaker, workshop leader, and life coach. Formerly he was an itinerant laborer, golf professional, pool hustler, airline executive, founding partner of an event and promotional marketing company, an Irish rogue wanderer, a yoga teacher, a somatic (body-centered) educator, and a seeker. He is dedicated to supporting people in transition—individuals and organizations called to inner transformation, mindfulness, and healing. A Canadian, Sean lives in rural New England, close to his beloved son, Beau. He is currently at work on another book of stories and poems.

For information about life coaching services or to book Sean as a speaker, visit his web site www.seanleclaire.com or call 978-369-6031.

Order Form

QUANTITY   AMOUNT

_____ *Hug an Angry Man and You Will*   _____
                See He Is Crying ($14.95)

Sales tax of 5% for Massachusetts residents   _____

                    Shipping & handling:
                    $2.50 per book   _____

                Total amount enclosed   _____

Method of payment
Check or money order enclosed (made payable to
Red Spiral Books in US currency only)

Please contact your local bookstore or mail your order, together
with your name, address, and check, or money order, to:

RED SPIRAL BOOKS
PO Box 1101
Concord, MA 01742
Phone: 978-369-6031
www.seanleclaire.com